ANTONIO
GAUDI

ANTONIO GAUDÍ

MASTER ARCHITECT

JUAN BASSEGODA NONELL

PHOTOGRAPHS BY MELBA LEVICK

ABBEVILLE PRESS PUBLISHERS

NEW YORK • LONDON

FRONT JACKET: Roof of the Casa Milà, on the right, one of the stairway exits and, on the left, the chimney added in 1956 by the architect Barba Corsini along with the construction of several duplex apartments in the attic. This chimney was eliminated in the restoration of 1992.

BACK JACKET: Windows in the facade of the Casa Batlló.

PAGE 1: Doorway tympanum of the Palacio Güell.

PAGE 2: Spiral staircase in a tower of the Sagrada Familia.

EDITOR: Susan Costello

DESIGNER: Paula Winicur

PRODUCTION MANAGER: Louise Kurtz

TRANSLATOR: Jeanne D'Andrea

MAP: Sophie Kittredge

First edition

10 9 8 7 6 5 4 3

Library of Congress Cataloging-in-Publication Data

Bassegoda Nonell, Juan.
    Antonio Gaudí/text by Juan Bassegoda Nonell: photography by Melba Levick.
        p.   Cm.
    Includes bibliographical reference and index.
    ISBN 0-7892-0220-4
    1. Gaudí Antoní 1852-1926—Criticism and interpretation. 2. Eclecticism in architecture—Spain.   I.   Title
NA1313.G3B26   2000
720'.92—dc21   97-38694
                                    CIP

CONTENTS

INTRODUCTION

THE WORK OF Antonio Gaudí Cornet (1852–1926) has transcended time, styles, and the period in which it was created. His achievement grew from his great capacity for observation and his fervent interest in nature. He was a passionate observer, learning directly from what he saw in the sky and the clouds, in water, rocks, plants, animals, and mountains.

To understand Gaudí's achievement one must recognize that his work is not exclusively architectural. It is more than that: it is not architectural in the sense that historians understand architecture. Gaudí's work does not fit into traditional schemes that would place it within the narrow limits of a particular style, nor was he the outstanding disciple of any master.

There had never been architects in the Gaudí family, only craftsmen, especially copper and iron smiths. He did not have the occupational idiosyncrasy that is characteristic of dynasties of architects. While he was extremely naive, he was also highly perspicacious. He saw things as they actually are, without prejudice, not as sometimes one might wish them to be. Juan Munné, a carpenter who worked with him for many years, said of him: "Gaudí is clear-minded." Throughout his career Gaudí made use of practical solutions that were both simple and functional, and through them he achieved surprising results.

Observing Gaudí's architectural forms, one might think that his was either a complex or a convoluted mind. The sinuous facades of his buildings look like somewhat irrational, baroque conceptions. But this is not the case. Because his compositions are inspired by nature, they stand out from those of architects who have always utilized a simple geometry based on abstract forms, like the line or the plane, forms that are nonexistent in nature.

In a logical process of simplification and abstraction, architects have developed designs and constructed buildings using only two auxiliary tools: the compass and the square. They have made use of these tools for drawing on a flat surface as well as for cutting stone or wood. From the plane and the straight line, both two-dimensional forms, one moves to three-dimensional forms, the regular polyhedrons, the cube, tetrahedron, octahedron, icosahedron, and pentagonal dodecahedron, forms that have been traditionally sanctified and identified with the elements of earth, fire, water, air, and the quintes-

7

Bench decorated with glazed tiles in the Park Güell.

PAGE 6: Doorway of the Casa Milà.

PAGE 7: Keystone of a vault in the hypostyle hall of the Park Güell. Glass and ceramic work by J. M. Jujol.

sential, as proposed by Plato in his *Timaeus* and developed by his followers. If these forms can be drawn with a square, the compass serves for drawing circles and spheres, forms that have always been used by architects.

In the architecture of every age, made with the help of a compass and square, all pillars can be described as prisms, all columns cylinders, all domes hemispheres, and all roofs dihedral angles or pyramids. This last form, so much loved by architects, is found from the pharonic pyramids of Giza built several thousand years ago to the recent courtyard entrance of the Louvre in Paris by I. M. Pei.

Gaudí's ingenuous observation of nature led him to see that these regular forms either do not exist in nature or, if they do, only rarely. When pyrite cubes are found, or prisms crowned with rock crystal, or pentagonal dodecahedrons of cinnabar, they are kept in museums of natural history as rare and curious objects.

In the light of the country landscape of Tarragona, Gaudí was moved by the beauty of natural forms. He was able to contemplate them at leisure during the summers spent in a little country house in the village of Riudoms. There, he observed that nature produces beautiful, decorative forms in the mineral, animal, and plant realms. At the same time, he understood that nature did not intend to create works of art but rather elements that were above all functional and useful. The brilliant color and agreeable fragrance of roses is not devised to inspire poets or painters but rather to attract insects and to encourage the reproductive function of the plant. An absolutely functional purpose. When Gaudí used the forms of plants, flowers, or animals in the decoration of his buildings, he took the natural forms just as they are in reality and not with the intention of so many architects over the course of history who have used them as an artistic intellectualization, submitting them to symmetries, dissymmetries, or compositional artifices.

Gaudí's conclusion was a very simple one. If an architect looks for the functional in his work, he will ultimately arrive at beauty. If he looks for beauty directly, he will only reach art theory, aesthetics, or philosophy, abstract ideas that never interested Gaudí. Moreover, he was able to see an infinity of magnificent structural forms in nature. If nature works by always looking for final solutions, since it is subject to the inexorable law of gravity, there is great wisdom in studying natural structures, which have been accredited by millions of years of perfect functioning. Knowing the essence of these structures, Gaudí sought to bring them to the arena of building.

He observed that in nature many structures are composed of fibrous materials, such as wood, bone, muscle, or tendon. From the viewpoint of geometry, fibers are straight lines and curved surfaces in space made up of straight lines that define a straight-line geometry, which is based on just four distinct surfaces: the helicoid, the hyperboloid, the conoid, and the hyperbolic paraboloid. Gaudí saw these surfaces in nature and brought them to architecture.

The helicoid is the form of a tree trunk, and Gaudí used this form in the columns of the Teresian School. The hyperboloid is the form of the femur, a form he used in the columns of the Sagrada Familia. The conoid is a form frequently found in the leaves of trees, and this form he used in the roofs of the Provisional Schools of the Sagrada Familia. The hyperbolic paraboloid is formed by the tendons between the fingers of the hand, and he built with this form the porch domes of the church crypt in the Güell Estate.

Gaudí had an innate sense of statics, which manifested itself in a simple, logical manner in the stereostatic model for the church of the Güell Estate. Once the ground floor of the church was drawn to a scale of 1:10 on a wooden panel, it was placed on the workshop ceiling and cords were suspended from it at the points where the pillars were assumed to begin. Hung above the catenaries formed by the cords were canvas sacks containing lead shot that weighed ten thousand times less than the weight the arch would have to support. The sacks of lead shot produced a warping of the cords. A photograph was then made of the inverted model. The photograph yielded the absolutely precise and exact form of the building's

The second viaduct in the Park Güell, built with stone from the site.

Bellesguard roof and tower with the double crucifix.

structure, with no need for mathematical calculations or drawings of any kind and with no possibility of error. The shapes of the cords corresponded to the lines of tension of the warped structure, and when the photograph was inverted the structure's lines of pressure were obtained. This simple, exact method attracted the attention of engineers and designers.

All of Gaudí's architecture is created by these intuitive, elemental methods, which permitted him to achieve equilibrated forms very like those found in nature. The bell towers of the Sagrada Familia are revolving paraboloids, and they correspond to the forms wet sand adopts when dropped from a height: they are perfectly balanced arrangements based on the law of gravity.

Gaudí believed that an architect must have an innate sense of equilibrium. The architect conceives the structure of a building and then passes its form on to the engineer who calculates the form mathematically. If the engineer pronounces the structure stable, all goes well; if he does not, Gaudí used to say, the architect must change, not his design but his profession. He would better dedicate himself to the theater or to politics, but not to building.

Moreover, Gaudí had a great advantage over other architects. As a child he was trained to be an iron smith in the forge of an uncle in Reus. After that, in the workshop of Eudaldo Puntí in Barcelona, he became familiar with carpentry, iron casting, and modeling in plaster. This training enabled him later to direct his workmen in logical ways that were easily understood. He always relied on the same workmen, and when they grew old and retired he trained others.

He did not like to draw his designs but rather to build models. He always used traditional techniques and achieved surprising results with them. In many of his buildings he made use of the *bóveda tabicada*, or Catalan vault, a timbrel-vault construction system that had been in frequent use since the fifteenth century, a slender shell vault formed by only two or three layers of brick joined with plaster or mortar at their small faces. By means of this procedure he not only constructed vaults in the forms of hyperbolic paraboloids or hyperboloids but also created a sculptural three-dimensionality that was totally new. The chimneys and ventilators as well as the stairway exits of the Casa Milà, forms of great sculptural beauty, were all built in this way, as were the roofs of Bellesguard and the Casa Batlló.

Fortunately, Gaudí had an extraordinary Maecenas in Don Eusebio Güell (from 1910, the Count of Güell), who allowed Gaudí to develop his ideas in absolute freedom. Güell became acquainted with Gaudí's work through a simple showcase design exhibited in 1878 at the Universal Exposition in Paris. Returning to Barcelona, Güell searched out the author of the design. From that time until Güell's death in 1918, he and Gaudí were inseparable. Their friendship of more than forty years was much more than a relationship between client and architect. In 1906 each went to live in his own respective house in the Park Güell, and there they were in contact on an almost daily basis. For Eusebio Güell, Gaudí designed the pavilions of the Güell Estate (1884–1887), the Palacio Güell (1886–1888), the Güell Cellars (1895–1897), the Crypt of the Güell Estate Church (1908–1917), the Park Güell (1900–1914), and other smaller works.

The architect reached exquisite extremes of purity in his architecture of straight-line geometry in his retreat at the Sagrada Familia. There he received many visitors to whom he explained his architectural theories. Gaudí began to direct the work on the Sagrada Familia in 1883, and he continued this work until June 7, 1926, three days before his death from an accident in which he was struck down by a streetcar.

Some of Gaudí's sayings were collected by young architects who admired the master's work, including Juan Bergós, César Martinell, J. F. Ràfols, and Isidro Puig Boada. A number of them are worth quoting:

"Wisdom is superior to science, it comes from 'sapere' or to savor; it refers to the concrete act. Elegance is the sister of poverty, but one must not confuse poverty with misery."

Patio of light in the Casa Batlló.

The interior of the stable roof at the Güell Estate displaying catenary arches and brick vaults.

"Art, which is masculine, nurtures science which is feminine. Sight is the sense of Glory, hearing is the sense of Faith. The ideal quality of a work of art is harmony, which in the visual arts comes from light that gives relief and decorates. Architecture is the ordering of light."

Most of Gaudí's remarks were collected by his followers, since Gaudí was not fond of writing. He published only one article during his lifetime, but he was very talkative and liked to explain the church of the Sagrada Familia to visiting groups. On Sunday mornings he customarily attended Mass in the cathedral and then took a long walk as far as the lighthouse on the cliff at the harbor. His usual companion was the architect Juan Bergós, who wrote down many excerpts from the maestro's long monologues, which he was not able to interrupt. César Martinell often visited Gaudí in his workshop and recorded some of his most interesting remarks. All of these were collected in the book *The Thinking of Gaudí (El pensament de Gaudí)* (1976) by Puig Boada. Ràfols worked in Gaudí's office in the church of the Sagrada Familia for more than two years, and in 1929 he published the first biography of the master. In it he reproduced many of the drawings from the Gaudí archive that was burned by the Anarchists in July 1936.

References to Gaudí's youth are very scarce. We have only the certificate of his baptism in the church of Saint Peter in Reus, dated June 26, 1852; his grades from the school where he received his secondary school diploma; and his academic record from Barcelona's School of Architecture where he obtained his title of architect on March 15, 1878.

Gaudí remained a bachelor until his death, living with his family until he remained alone late in his life. As a student, he shared lodgings in inexpensive inns with his brother Francisco, a medical student. After that, he lived with his father and his orphan niece, Rosa Egea Gaudí, first in several different houses in Barcelona and then from 1906 onward in the Park Güell house, the model house that had never been purchased. There, his father died, at ninety-three, in 1906 and his niece Rosa in 1912.

Good friends of Gaudí's youthful years included Eduardo Toda, who became a diplomat; José Ribera, later a professor of medicine; the sculptor Lorenzo Matamala; and the architect Juan Martorell. Martorell was a great help to Gaudí because he introduced him to the study of graphic statics, which at the time was not taught at the School of Architecture. In addition, he recommended Gaudí as architect for the Sagrada Familia and introduced him to the Comillas and the Güell families. Gaudí used to say of Martorell that he was both a wise man and a saint. Gaudí received two decisive lessons in his life from Martorell: an acquaintance with Neogothic architecture and an introduction to graphic statics. The first lesson enabled him to understand the medieval style, which was eminently applicable to building, and the second enabled him to go beyond Gothic solutions and penetrate the world of equilibrated forms.

When Gaudí assumed the supervision of the project at the Sagrada Familia in 1883 through Martorell's influence, he encountered a strictly Neogothic structure begun the year before by the architect Francisco Villar Lozano, who had initiated work on the crypt. In his first design, signed in March 1885, Gaudí worked in the manner of Martorell, but eight years later he had already formalized in theory his general idea of the new church with its absolutely original forms. From 1890 until his death in 1926, Gaudí prepared four distinct solutions for the structure, each time further refining the style and the ingenious static arrangement. He made plaster models in several scales of the entire temple and of its details. Although these models were destroyed in July 1936, their reconstruction has enabled Gaudí's successors to continue his work at the church.

Gaudí had many admirers in his own time, but he never concerned himself with publicizing his work. In 1910 Eusebio Güell spent a sizable sum mounting a large-scale Gaudí exhibition at the Grand Palais in Paris. Filling the entire ground floor of the building were models, drawings, and photographs of Gaudí's work. But Gaudí refused to go to Paris, and the exhibition was celebrated without him. His vocation was exclusively archi-

Central drawing room of the Palacio Güell, *calle Nou de la Rambla, 3.*

The Nativity facade of the Sagrada Familia.

tectural, indeed his entire life was devoted to architecture. He never married, he did not write (except for his article of 1881), he rarely traveled, he did not become involved in politics. His only diversion was his beloved architecture.

Gaudí was a shy, ingenuous man of great sensitivity, capable of understanding architectural forms by observing nature. Very attached to his native region and his family, he retained the Catalan accent of the Reus area all his life, and he believed that that part of Catalonia was ideal for artistic creation. Jan Molema, the Dutch engineer who has studied Gaudí, commented that the architect believed that the nearer to Reus a person was born the more intelligent that person was. Putting exaggeration aside, Gaudí in truth thought that the Mediterranean basin was the optimal birthplace for works of art. The light there falls at about 45 degrees and illuminates objects perfectly, so that they can be seen without the slightest distortion. Mediterranean people, according to Gaudí, are synthetists, just as Northerners are analysts. Analysis is necessary for understanding the secrets of the world, but artistic creation requires synthesis.

His great love for the landscape and terrain of the Mediterranean countries grew as it was filtered through his religious spirit. He loved nature in the same way that Saint Francis of Assisi had loved it. If nature is the work of God and architectural forms are derived from nature, this means that the work of the Creator is being continued. Gaudí said that God continued the Creation through man, and he tried to be worthy of this creative act. His religiosity was active and he did not limit himself to following the advice of ecclesiastics. He often entered into discussions with them, although generally he settled for the friendship of distinguished churchmen, like the bishops of Vic, Mallorca, and Astorga.

Gaudí liked to discuss liturgical subjects, but he chose to avoid conversations on theology. He always preferred the concrete to the abstract. His architecture is highly poetic, but he disliked written poetry. He said that verse gave him a headache, but this did not rule out his friendships with poets such as Fr. Jacinto Verdaguer or Francesch Matheu.

Gaudí always expressed himself through architecture. In his doctoral thesis on Gaudí, the Taiwanese architect Hou Teh-Chien maintains that Gaudí realized a metaphoric architecture, that he was a philosopher who expressed his ideas by constructing buildings. Gaudí did not read books on philosophy or architecture. He assiduously read "L'Année Liturgique," by the Abbot of Solesmes, Dom Guéranger, a liturgical calendar that explained the religious feasts and the ways of celebrating them. Asked once what his favorite architectural treatise was, Gaudí gestured through his studio window saying that the tree outside was his favorite book on architecture.

His architectural production is limited to a small number of buildings, although the Sagrada Familia alone is much more than a building. Since 1969, seventeen of his works have become national monuments in Spain and they are protected by law. Gaudí was given to constantly perfecting his works, never considering them finished. Moreover, he constructed a building integrally, from its foundation and structural framework to the smallest decorative and ornamental detail. He designed furniture, windows, wrought iron accessories, and every type of auxiliary element, never repeating any model. Each Gaudí building has its own special characteristics and looks like none of the others. Each was conceived in its integrity and constitutes a unity in which all of the elements are perfectly coordinated and exclusive to that building.

When Gaudí died in 1926, the new Bauhaus building designed by Walter Gropius had just been erected. This was the culminating moment of rationalism, of Le Corbusier, Siegfried Giedion, and the Congrès Internationaux d'Architecture Moderne. This architecture of simple geometric forms, of purely abstract conception, was at odds with the work of Gaudí, which was considered baroque and irrational.

The next generation of architects continued to understand gaudian thought in a similar way, and it was not until the Gaudí exhibition of 1952, on the centenary of his birth, that critics and scholarly writers began to discover the value of his architecture. The flood of books, articles,

Coronation of the Virgin, Nativity Portal of the Sagrada Familia.

The Casa Batlló illuminated, showing the
colored glass decoration.

courses, lectures, and enthusiasm for Gaudí came later. But those least interested in Gaudí have been the architects who, inspired by the work of the reputed masters, have repeated their solutions a thousand and one times.

Gaudí presents the problem of an inimitable personality, and all the attempts that have been made to imitate him have failed.

Looking toward the future, the lesson of Gaudí is not to copy his solutions but rather to look at nature for inspiration. There is such a variety of solutions in natural forms that there is never a risk of repetition. Gaudí found amazing structures by working in a rational, logical way and, moreover, in a timeless fashion. Unlike historic styles, nature does not go out of fashion.

During the Roman era, oaks, cypresses, and ilexes grew around the temples. When the great Gothic works were built, the oaks, cypresses, and ilexes continued to grow around them. Today, surrounding the buildings of steel and glass, the same trees still grow. They continue to give us pleasure because we never tire of nature.

One never becomes tired of the architecture of Gaudí, because he looked directly to nature for solutions. His work continues to delight us today, just as it did when he was alive. It is an architecture beyond time, because he did not propose to make art but rather to make functional and useful forms.

Gaudí's famous phrase, originality is returning to the origin, means that the origin of all things is nature, created by God.

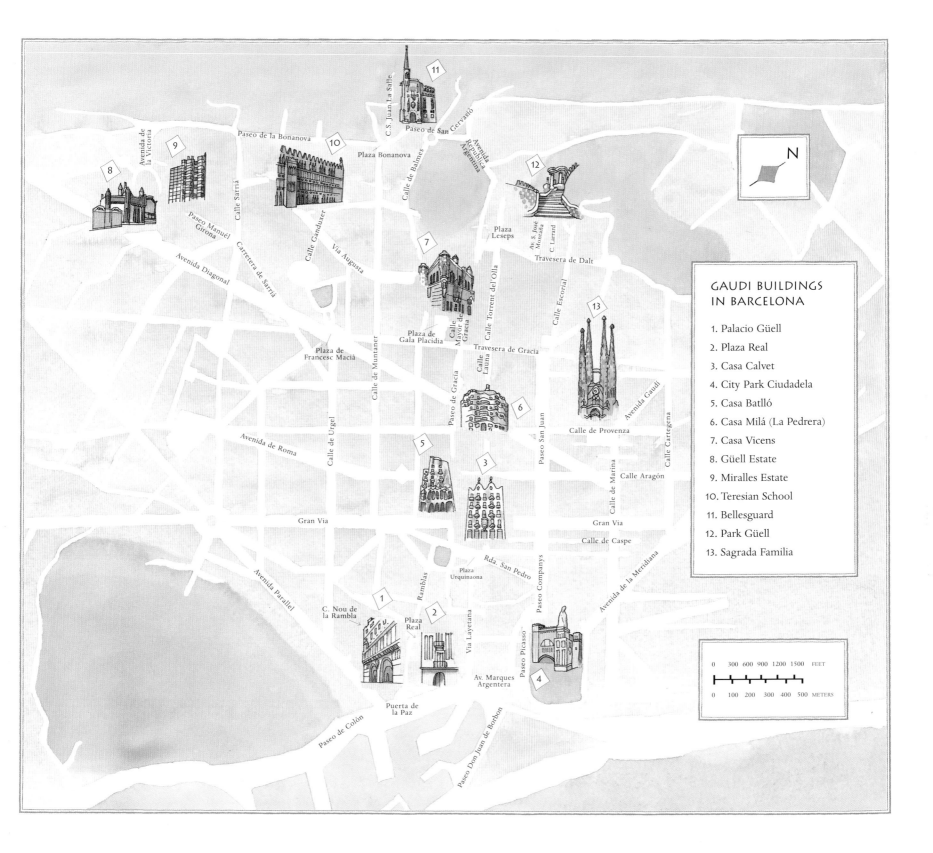

N

Paseo de la Bonanova

Avenida de la Victoria

Paseo Manuél Girona

Calle Sarriá

Carretera de Sarriá

Avenida Diagonal

Calle Ganduxer

Via Augusta

C.S. Juan La Salle

Paseo de San Gervasió

Calle de Balmes

Avenida República Argentina

Plaza Bonanova

Plaza Leseps

Av. S. José Montaña

C. Larrard

Travesera de Dalt

Calle Escorial

Calle Torrent del Olla

Plaza de Gala Placidia

Calle Mayor de Gracia

Travesera de Gracia

Plaza de Francesc Macià

Calle de Muntaner

Calle Lauria

Paseo de Gracia

Paseo San Juan

Calle de Urgel

Avenida de Roma

Gran Via

Calle de Provenza

Avenida Gaudi

Calle de Marina

Calle Aragón

Calle Cartegena

Gran Via

Calle de Caspe

Rda. San Pedro

Plaza Urquinaona

Avenida de la Meridiana

Ramblas

Via Layetana

Paseo Companys

C. Nou de la Rambla

Plaza Real

Av. Marques Argentera

Paseo Picasso

Avenida Parallel

Puerta de la Paz

Paseo de Colón

Paseo Don Juan de Borbon

GAUDI BUILDINGS IN BARCELONA

1. Palacio Güell
2. Plaza Real
3. Casa Calvet
4. City Park Ciudadela
5. Casa Batlló
6. Casa Milá (La Pedrera)
7. Casa Vicens
8. Güell Estate
9. Miralles Estate
10. Teresian School
11. Bellesguard
12. Park Güell
13. Sagrada Familia

0   300 600 900 1200 1500   FEET

0   100 200 300 400 500   METERS

EARLY WORK

GAUDÍ BEGAN HIS architectural studies at the University of Barcelona in 1869. Economic constraints obliged him to work as a draftsman for a number of different architects and for the master builder José Fontserè Mestres, director of works for the new *Park of the Ciudadela*. Working in the eclectic style of the time, Gaudí designed the balustrade of the plaza that was later named Aribau and the iron fence that encloses the park area. He also collaborated on the design of the metal structure for the Borne market and made a drawing for a fountain in the center of the market. Unfortunately, the drawing was destroyed, although both designs and photographs survive.

In the course of his studies, Gaudí made a series of designs for required subjects. The coloration and exquisiteness of his watercolor drawings are remarkable. Among these designs are a cemetery arch, a large fountain for the Plaza Cataluña, a patio for a public building, a wharf, and, as a final project, a university assembly hall.

Beginning in 1873, Gaudí collaborated on the construction of housing, a factory workers' club, and a machine shop for the *Mataró*

Cooperative, the first complex of its kind to be established in Spain. The cooperative was based on the idea of a worker-owned factory, a concept that interested Gaudí and was consonant with his youthful ideas on social problems. He also designed the company's banner, and in 1885 he directed the decoration of the factory shop for a large celebration for the workers' families, converting the shop's interior into a forest that caused a great stir at the event.

In 1878 Gaudí received an assignment from the Barcelona city council to design two models for gas street lamps, to be located on the principal streets and plazas of the city. One of the two prototypes had three branches and the other six. He combined a stone base with a cast iron and bronze shaft and branches and lamps of opaline glass. In an extensive report, Gaudí demonstrated that he had thoroughly studied the gas lighting systems of the world's great cities. Ultimately, only two gas lamps with six branches were installed in the *Plaza Real* and two with three branches in the Plaza de Palacio.

Although Gaudí's work of this initial period is very exceptional, it does not yet reflect his own personal style.

19

Student Drawings

◆

BARCELONA

◆

1873-1877

PAGE 18: Fountain in the Park of the Ciudadela. By José Fontserè (1829–1887) with the assistance of Gaudí.

PAGE 19: Balustrade detail in the Plaza Aribau.

ABOVE: Student drawing by Gaudí, a design for a Royal Wharf, 1876.

RIGHT: Design detail for a university assembly hall (Paraninfo Universitario). Project for final examinations.

FAR RIGHT: Design detail for the Provincial Government Offices (Diputación), 1876.

OPPOSITE: Iron gate by Gaudí at the entrance to the Park of the Ciudadela, 1875.

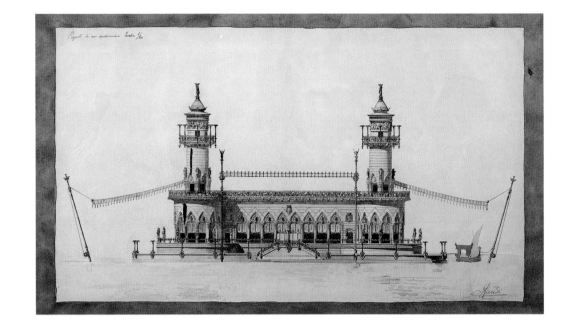

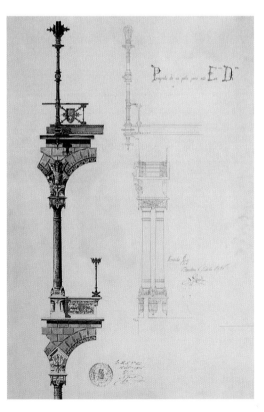

Park of the Ciudadela

BARCELONA

1875-1878

OPPOSITE, LEFT: Iron fence
in the Park of the
Ciudadela. Fabricated in
the workshops of
La Nueva Vulcano.

OPPOSITE, TOP RIGHT:
Street lamps on the iron
fence of the Park of the
Ciudadela.

OPPOSITE, BOTTOM RIGHT:
Warrior's helmet on the
iron fence of the
Ciudadela.

LEFT: Detail of the
balustrade of the
Plaza Aribau.

Mataró Cooperative • MATARÓ (BARCELONA) • 1873-1885

Factory of the Mataró Cooperative with wood framing.

Plaza Real • BARCELONA • 1878-1879

Street lamp of cast iron and stone in the Plaza Real, 1879

EASTERN INFLUENCE

A TREND IN architectural style that combined the Neogothic with the exotic began to develop in Europe during the last quarter of the nineteenth century. In Spain some architects looked to foreign schools of architecture for inspiration. Luis Domènech Montaner and José Vilaseca Casanovas were attracted to German architecture, which was in the ascendancy after the Franco-Prussian War. Gaudí, who had read Walter Pater and John Ruskin, looked to the exoticism of English architecture as well as to the Far East, especially to the architecture of India, Persia, and Japan.

Four extant youthful works show Gaudí's clear interest in the Far East. *El Capricho* (1883–1885), in Northern Spain on the shore of the Cantábrico Sea in the town of Comillas, is a building formerly covered in glass tiles, with a tall, slender cylindrical tower that resembles a minaret from Isfahan. El Capricho does not yet display technical innovations, but it represents a step forward in his personal style.

The *Casa Vicens* (1883–1888), in the Barcelona suburb of Gracia, also partakes of these Eastern forms, especially in its use of glass tiles. In this project, Gaudí introduces the use of the catenary arch in the garden waterfall and naturalism in the grill-work with cast-iron palm leaves. For the house, he also studied furniture design and interior decoration using papier-mâché in vivid colors.

For the *Güell Estate* (1884–1887), on the outskirts of Barcelona, Gaudí constructed among other elements the porter's house, the stables, and the riding ring at the entrance to the extensive park surrounding the house of Don Eusebio Güell. The exteriors of these structures have a brilliant oriental look, thanks to their ceramic embellishments, but the interiors offer new structural forms: arches and vaults with catenary profiles and hyperbolic domes.

The *Palacio Güell* (1886–1888), in the ancient quarter of Barcelona, is an overwhelming work, with many new solutions to the structuring and distribution of spaces and volumes, combined with an equal measure of Eastern influences. Some of the decoration is by Gaudí, although the painters Alejo Clapés and Alejandro de Riquer and the architect Camilo Oliveras also were involved.

El Capricho · COMILLAS · 1883-1885

Casa Vicens

BARCELONA

1883-1888

PAGE 26: Facade of the Casa Vicens, *calle Carolinas, 24.*

PAGE 27: Doorway lamp of the Casa Vicens.

OPPOSITE: Built for Don Máximo de Quijano and displaying stone, brick, and glazed tiles on the facade.

RIGHT: Detail of a chimney.

OPPOSITE: Corner tower.

LEFT: Door in the stone and ceramic facade.

ABOVE: Balcony. The iron railing is not by Gaudí.

OPPOSITE: Corner balcony with terra-cotta sculptures by Riba García.

ABOVE: Tile with a Moorish-carnation *(Tagetes patula)* motif.

LEFT: Leaded-glass windows in the vestibule.

OPPOSITE, LEFT: Dining room with furniture designed by Gaudí and paintings by Jose Torrescasana.

OPPOSITE, RIGHT: Dining room fireplace displaying incised and painted ceramic decorations.

LEFT: Smoking room with painted plaster vault and walls covered with tiles and papier-mâché stones.

PAGES 36–37: Entrance gate with a wrought-iron dragon and walls of stone, brick, and stucco.

PAGE 37, TOP: Porter's house and garden railing.

PAGE 37, BOTTOM: Stuccoed adobe walls of the stables, with painted and perforated surfaces.

Güell Estate • BARCELONA • 1884-1887

OPPOSITE: Ventilator of the porter's house decorated with tiles.

LEFT: Bell at the entrance of the Güell Estate.

ABOVE: Detail of the pedestrian door of the estate.

PAGE 40: Balustrade of brick and tile in the stables.

LEFT: Orange tree, made of antimony on the sustaining column of the doorway, represents the Garden of the Hesperides.

OPPOSITE: Ground floor facade.

ABOVE: Coat of arms of Catalonia,
made of wrought iron.

RIGHT: Bay on the rear facade.

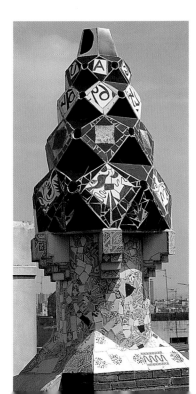

OPPOSITE: Upper part of the facade and roof terrace.

LEFT: Chimneys and ventilators after the last restoration.

BELOW LEFT: Restored chimney.

BELOW CENTER: Upper part of finial and weathervane.

BELOW RIGHT: Chimney. The ceramic decoration is not by Gaudí.

PAGE 46: Interior of the central drawing room.

PAGE 47: Coffered ceiling of a first floor room.

NEOGOTHICISM

GAUDÍ HAD BOTH a protector and a colleague in the architect Juan Martorell Montells (1833–1906), a very religious man who built churches and convents in the Neogothic style of the era, following the ideas of the architect and theorist-writer Viollet-le-Duc. Gaudí collaborated with Martorell on several projects and learned this style from him. Gaudí believed the Gothic was the most structural of historic styles. Renaissance architects, he said, are merely decorators. After studying Gothic buildings, he conceived a way of perfecting medieval structural solutions. Toward the end of the nineteenth century, he made a series of designs in the Neogothic idiom of Martorell. Gaudí decorated the chapel of the schools of nuns at Saint Andrew of Palomar (Barcelona) (1880) and *The School of Jesus-Mary* in Tarragona (1879) with altars, and choir stalls that were purely Neogothic. In this style too is the design for the chapel of the Holy Sacrament in the parish church of Saint Fèlix of Alella (1883), although the work was not realized. For Don José Bocabella, who promoted the construction of the church of the Sagrada Familia, he designed a Neogothic altar of carved wood.

In 1887 Gaudí was charged with completing the *Teresian School* for nuns in San Gervasio, begun by another architect. Gaudí subsequently modified the initial design but was unable to alter the building's rectangular form, since the first floor had already been built.

The structure was crowned with battlements appropriate to a medieval fortress, but the elegant, well-composed ensembles of brick catenary arches of its interior produced a strongly inspired, absolutely novel effect.

In 1887 he also began to design the palace of the bishop of Astorga (León), a Catalan who had been in touch with Gaudí for many years. This building was made of granite, and its original composition has a strong Gothic character, especially in the ogival vaults of the ground and first floors. Gaudí abandoned supervision of the work in 1893, and the present roofs do not correspond to the original design.

While he was working at Astorga, Gaudí was engaged to do a business and apartment block in León, the *Casa de los Botines* (Casa Fernández y Andrés; 1891–1892), situated on the Plaza de San Marcelo. Built of limestone, it is Neogothic in its lines with a very original roof system of slate. At the basement and ground levels were the shops and offices of a textile business.

Bellesguard (1900–1909) is a different case. It is an isolated building on a slope of the Collserola mountains, in a place once occupied by a medieval summer house belonging to King Martin I of Aragon. As a memorial to the king, Gaudí conceived a work inspired by the Catalan Gothic style of the fifteenth century, although he introduced daring new structural solutions.

School of
Jesus-Mary

TARRAGONA

1879

PAGE 48: Episcopal Palace of
Astorga, León, 1889–1893.
Constructed of granite
from El Bierzo in north-
western Spain.

PAGE 49: Lamp by
Domingo Sugrañes.
Bellesguard.

LEFT: Altar of the
school chapel.

OPPOSITE: Design for the
Casa de los Botines.

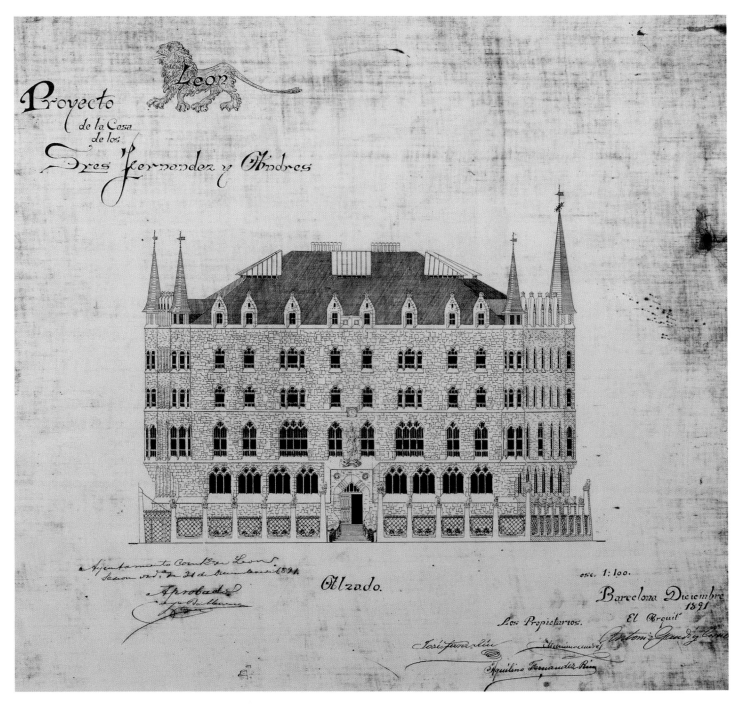

Facade of the Teresian School.

ABOVE: Detail of the bay and crenellation.

RIGHT: Wrought-iron entrance gate.

ABOVE: Coat of arms of the Carmelite Order in the bay.

LEFT: Wood and glass door.

OPPOSITE: Brick catenary arches around
the first floor patio.

ABOVE: Columns of single-brick thickness
on the first floor.

RIGHT: Hall and patio of lights
on the ground floor.

Bellesguard

•

BARCELONA

•

1900-1909

OPPOSITE: Casa Bellesguard. Brick
walls covered with slate.

ABOVE: Tympanum of the entrance door
inscribed with "the Hail Mary."

RIGHT: Mosaic bench by Domingo Sugrañes.

Brick arches of the attic.

ABOVE, LEFT: Stairwell of the house.

ABOVE, RIGHT: Stairway showing plastered brick vaulting. Ceramic dado by Domingo Sugrañes.

OPPOSITE: Slate roofs of the attic.

LEFT: Lateral facade overlooking the garden.

ABOVE: Metal door of the coach house.

NATURALISM

GAUDÍ'S MOST CREATIVE period corresponds to the completely free development of his ideas based on an architecture inspired by nature. Understanding that in nature there is no straight line or plane and that by contrast there is an immense variety of curved forms, he changed the normal procedure of designing on a plane surface and launched directly into the third dimension, making use of every kind of model. He made them of wood, plaster, clay, metal screening, wet cardboard, and wire.

Gaudí's love of nature was based on his attentive, naive observation of the forms of plants, animals, and mountains. He admired the beauty of all these forms, recognizing that nature's purpose is not aesthetic but functional. Nature does not try to make works of art but rather elements that rule the growth and reproduction of species. He concluded that in looking for function, one arrives at beauty, and that the direct search for beauty leads only to philosophy, aesthetics, or art theory. Gaudí was a simple man, an enemy of abstract ideas, a man who knew how to see the reality of things without prejudice or professional bias.

Among Gaudí's naturalistic works is the *Casa Calvet* (1898–1899). On the building's facade he placed a collection of mushrooms to please his patron, Señor Calvet, who was a micologist. The facade design was made first in the form of a plaster model to a scale of 1:10.

In the *Güell Cellars* (1895–1897), on the outskirts of Garraf, he erected a building in the locale's native stone, which is in perfect harmony with the rocky contour of the coast.

The concept of naturalism becomes more evident in the Park Güell (1900-1914). Here, the architect planned the streets to adapt to the rough topography, constructing viaducts so that the terrain's original contours were left unchanged. He built with the native stone and even took advantage of the ruins of a cave, distributing its rocks of different colors harmoniously throughout the grounds.

The *Casa Batlló* (1904–1906) and the *Casa Milà* (1906–1911) were the culmination of his naturalist architecture. The Casa Batlló, covered with pieces of colored glass ceramic, and the Casa Milà, with its cliff-like aspect, seem to be symbols of sea and earth. Other examples of this way of working can be seen in the stained glass of the *Cathedral of Mallorca* (1903–1914), in the Resurrection of Christ on the Mountain of Montserrat (1903–1916), and in other lesser works. Nature is reflected in Gaudí's architecture like trees on the surface of a lake.

Casa Calvet

BARCELONA

1898-1899

PAGE 62: Attic of the
Casa Milà, today
the Museo
Espai Gaudí.

PAGE 63: Ceramic
dragon's head on
the stairway of the
Park Güell.

RIGHT: Facade of
the Casa Calvet,
calle Caspe, 48.

LEFT: Iron cross on a stone sphere with its completion date, on the upper part of the facade.

ABOVE: Detail of the lower part of the facade.

OPPOSITE: Elevator cage in the stairwell.

FAR LEFT: Wrought-iron cupola of the elevator.

LEFT: Entrance hall door and ceramic paneling.

BELOW: Stairway railing of wrought iron and wood.

RIGHT: Peephole of cast bronze in an interior door.

FAR RIGHT: Office lamp on the ground floor.

BELOW: Oak table, armchair, and chair in the ground floor offices.

OPPOSITE: Fountain and planter on the rear terrace of the first floor.

OPPOSITE: Business offices on the ground floor.

LEFT: Wood and glass door to the offices.

Güell Cellars

Exterior view.

Cathedral of Mallorca

◆

MALLORCA

◆

1903-1914

LEFT: Baldachin of the principal altar.

ABOVE: Fragment of the
heptagonal baldachin.

OPPOSITE: Stairway, fountains, and Doric colonnade.

LEFT: Ceramic medallion on the stairway with the coat of arms of Catalonia and a dragon's head.

Park Güell ✦ BARCELONA ✦ 1900-1914

OPPOSITE & BELOW: On the stairway a dragon made of pieces of broken ceramics.

RIGHT: Ceramic mosaic below the bench of the Doric colonnade.

OPPOSITE: Side wall of the stairway with prefabricated sections of ceramic mosaic.

ABOVE: Side wall of the stairway and crenellation decorated with tile.

TOP: Crenellation decorated with a variety of glass mosaic.

ABOVE: Detail of the slightly curved wall flanking the stairway.

OPPOSITE: View of the garden and a tile-covered bench, on the first level.

ABOVE: Curving bench covered with broken tiles in the plaza of the Greek Theater.

RIGHT: The gently curving bench encloses the entire plaza.

ABOVE: Ceramic soffit in place of one of the four omitted columns in the Doric hypostyle hall below the plaza of the Greek Theater.

RIGHT: Vault keystone in the hypostyle hall. Ceramic and colored glass decoration by J. M. Jujol.

OPPOSITE: Doric colonnade below the plaza.

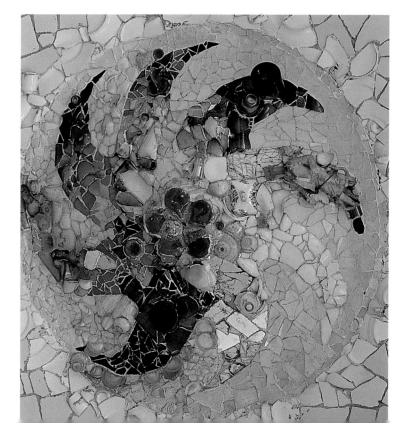

OPPOSITE: Upper part of the porter's house in the Park Güell.

LEFT: Ceramic-clad roof of the porter's house.

The Park Güell house, designed by Francisco Berenguer in 1902, where Gaudí lived from 1906 to 1925. Today the house is the Casa-Museo Gaudí.

LEFT: Entrance to the garden.

BELOW, LEFT: Rear facade of Gaudí's house.

BELOW: Stone portico in Gaudí's garden.

PAGE 88: First stone viaduct of the park's principal street.

PAGE 89: Calvary, or the hill of the three crosses, on the highest point of the Park Güell.

Miralles Estate ✦ BARCELONA ✦ 1900-1902

OPPOSITE: Entrance doorway where a newly installed, life-size bronze statue of Gaudí stands. It was sculpted by Joaquín Camps, whose grandfather, the sculptor, José María Camps Arnau, worked with Gaudí.

LEFT: Detail of the Miralles doorway.

ABOVE: Upper part of the doorway with the iron double crucifix.

Casa Batlló

•

BARCELONA

•

1904-1906

RIGHT: Facade of
the house,
paseo de Gracia, 43.

OPPOSITE: First floor
bay of carved
stone, wood, and
leaded glass.

OPPOSITE: Top of the facade made entirely of glazed ceramic.

LEFT: Rear terrace of the first floor.

BELOW LEFT: Detail of ceramic and broken-glass decoration on the rear terrace.

BELOW: Base of the terrace grille with ceramic disks and broken glass.

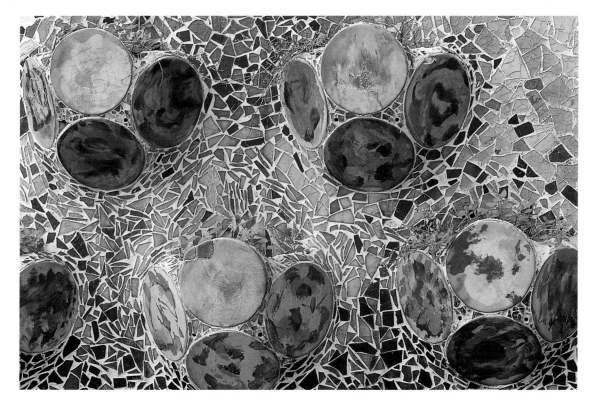

RIGHT: Attic roof and cross of Mallorcan ceramic atop the circular tower.

OPPOSITE, TOP LEFT: Roof terrace.

OPPOSITE, BOTTOM LEFT: View from the roof terrace of the chimneys, attic roof, and ceramic cross.

OPPOSITE, RIGHT: Detail of the chimneys covered with broken glass.

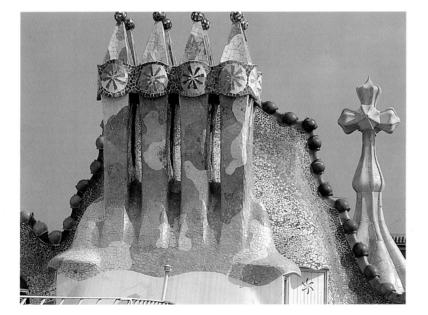

OPPOSITE: Vestibule and stairway on the ground floor.

ABOVE: Fireplace of refractory ceramic in the first floor anteroom.

Casa Milà • BARCELONA • 1906-1911

OPPOSITE: Casa Milà, *paseo de Gracia, 92,* is popularly known as *La Pedrera* (The Quarry).

LEFT: Stone facade and wrought-iron balcony balustrade.

PAGE 102: Foreshortened view of the beveled facade.

PAGE 103, LEFT: Detail of a wrought-iron balcony fabricated by José and Luis Badia.

PAGE 103, TOP RIGHT: Limestone and wrought iron are combined on this balcony.

PAGE 103, BOTTOM RIGHT: The wrought-iron design for each balcony is different, and none is repeated.

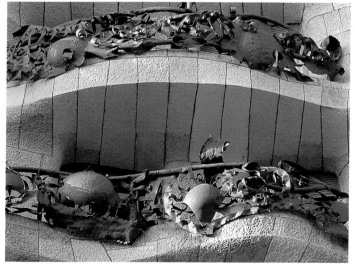

OPPOSITE: Patio and main floor stairway.

ABOVE: A vestibule with pictorial decoration by Alejo Clapés, Javier Nogués, Teresa Lostau, and Ivo Pascual.

LEFT: Simple balcony railing around the patio.

OPPPOSITE, LEFT: Glass
screen in the
porter's house.

OPPOSITE, RIGHT: Entrance
to the porter's house.

LEFT: Window on the
patio stairway.

RIGHT: First floor hallway.

OPPOSITE, TOP: Sculptured plaster ceiling on the first floor.

OPPOSITE, BOTTOM: Plaster ceiling reliefs on the first floor.

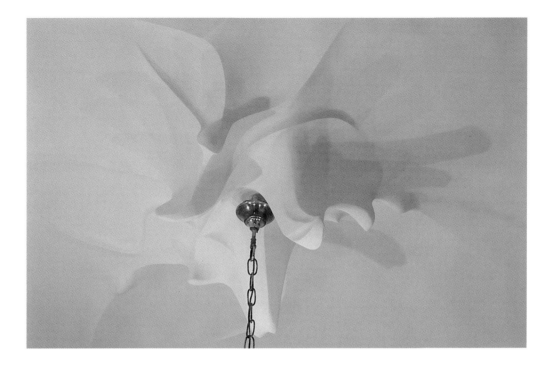

RIGHT: View from above of the circular patio.

OPPOSITE, TOP: The oval patio.

OPPOSITE, BOTTOM: Windows, balustrades, and painted walls of the circular patio.

OPPOSITE: Upper part of the facade and roof terrace.

ABOVE: Chimneys, ventilators, and stairway exits on the roof.

PAGE 114, TOP LEFT: Gaudí's design for the facade of the house, 1906.

PAGE 114, BOTTOM LEFT: Plan of the house signed by Gaudí and Milà, 1906.

PAGE 115: A night view of a stairway exit and a ventilator on the roof.

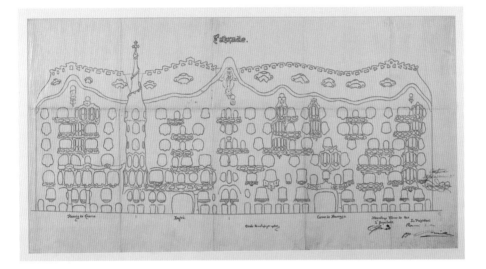

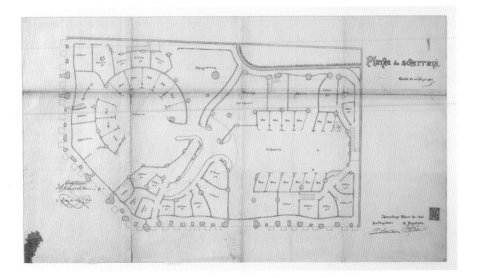

STRAIGHT-LINE GEOMETRY

1 9 0 8   1 9 1 7

GAUDÍ WAS NEVER able to understand why architects based their buildings on the simple geometry of line and plane and on regular solid forms, since such forms either do not exist, or exist only rarely, in nature. Nature, by contrast, makes extraordinary structures with fibrous elements that constitute bone, wood, muscle, and tendon—a geometry of straight lines in space forming four types of surfaces: helicoids, conoids, hyperboloids, and hyperbolic paraboloids. These are surfaces that are ubiquitous in nature and for this reason useful and functional, like a work by nature, surfaces that have scarcely been employed by architects.

The application of a straight-line geometry and the catenary arch, another mechanical and functional form that occurs often in nature, was constant in Gaudí's architecture. He initially used catenary arches, for example, in the stables of the Güell Estate and in the waterfall of the Casa Vicens, hyperboloids in the Palacio Güell columns, and hyperbolic paraboloids in the porter's house at the Park Güell. This type of geometry clearly manifests itself in two of his most significant works.

In 1909 Gaudí was commissioned to build a low-cost structure to house the *Provisional Schools of the Sagrada Familia* until the church was completed. Classrooms and workshops would then be located in the church half-basements. Using only Catalan brick vault construction—the *bóveda tabicada*, or board vault—he built a structure with undulating walls and roof, a roof composed of a conoid form joined by iron I-beams that served as directives. Using this system he erected a school with three classrooms at a minimal cost. This simple but highly inspired work by Gaudí has had wide dissemination among architects through Le Corbusier's drawing and commentaries made during his stay in Barcelona in 1928.

Nevertheless, full development of Gaudí's greatest geometric refinement occurs in the church of the Sagrada Familia. He reached this stage between 1916 and 1926, working with plaster models to a scale of 1:25 for the entire building and of 1:10 for the structure of the naves. These models were destroyed in 1936 and restored about 1939. Now on exhibition in the church museum, the models enable the understanding and completion of the work of converting the Sagrada Familia into an authentic school of architecture, where architects of different nationalities can work and study with the most advanced technology.

Gaudí's seclusion in the Sagrada Familia, with no desire to accept other commissions, can be explained by his personal interest in leaving his geometric-naturalist theory of architecture sufficiently developed for others to complete. He chose to focus on his master work and to open great possibilities for new generations of architects.

PAGE 116: Interior of the crypt of the Güell Estate Church in Santa Coloma de Cervelló (Barcelona), 1908–1917.

PAGE 117: Iron and colored-glass window in the crypt.

OPPOSITE: Stairway of the unfinished main church.

LEFT: Portico of the crypt seen from the stairway of the main church.

BELOW: Exterior of the crypt windows with iron grilles and colored glass.

OPPOSITE: Brick portico vaults in the form of hyperbolic paraboloids.

BELOW: Interior of the crypt with basalt columns, brick arches, and ribs

ABOVE: Brick columns adjacent to the chapel of Santo Cristo.

RIGHT: Basalt columns and colored-glass windows.

OPPOSITE: Schools of the Sagrada Familia, constructed entirely of brick with a roof in the form of a double conoid.

Handwritten note: Gaudí developed design at for Sagrada Familia being inspired by the requirements of his other clients "Tangiers" and "NY project"

edifi... ...would take several generations to complete. The Sagrada Familia is an analytical laboratory for studying the methods and solutions based on straight-line geometry and equilibrated structures.

But the process Gaudí followed to reach the forms he used in the work of the Sagrada Familia, especially during the last period of his life, between 1914 and 1926, began to take shape much earlier in two other designs that were not carried out but are of particular interest.

In 1892 the second Marquis of Comillas commissioned a design for the *Franciscan Catholic Missions* in Tangiers (Morocco) that would include a church, schools, and a hospital. Gaudí estimated that he could complete the project within a year. The idea was finally abandoned because the Franciscans found the building too large and luxurious. Its central tower would have soared to 1,968 feet (60 meters), and the axes of its quadrilobed plan extended to about 1,968 feet as well (60 x 60 meters). The inclined walls, hyperboloid windows, and revolving paraboloid towers were not built. However, the form intended for the Tangiers towers was put to use in the towers of the Sagrada Familia, which were begun in 1903. Gaudí was very disappointed by the failure to build the Tangiers mission, and when he next had a chance to design a large-scale building, he opted for equilibrated design solutions like those of the Tangiers design.

In 1908 he received a visit from two American entrepreneurs who engaged him to design a hotel in New York City. Gaudí imagined a building almost 9,843 feet (300 meters) tall with a catenary profile that would achieve a perfect structural equilibrium. The project was not carried out, surely because of an illness that left Gaudí extremely weak between 1901 and 1910.

These two unrealized experimental designs were magnificent incentives to advance toward the definitive forms of the Sagrada Familia. The elegant towers of the Tangiers design and the colossal daring of the New York project permitted Gaudí to realize the final structural model for the Sagrada Familia, refining to the utmost his studies of the straight-line surfaces of hyperboloids and hyperbolic paraboloids, and of the slender, rational, highly elegant shapes of the columns for the church's main nave.

In 1909, moreover, shortly after his interview with the American clients, he constructed the small building for the provisional parish school of the Sagrada Familia. Its roof is a board vault in the shape of a director-plane conoid, a highly stable and economical straight-line surface. With this solution he brought to a close his study of both small and gigantic forms, a study that extends from the school of the Sagrada Familia to the Tangiers design to the hotel for New York.

All of this became a splendid reality in the structural models for the Sagrada Familia, which were converted into a tangible reality after the master's death.

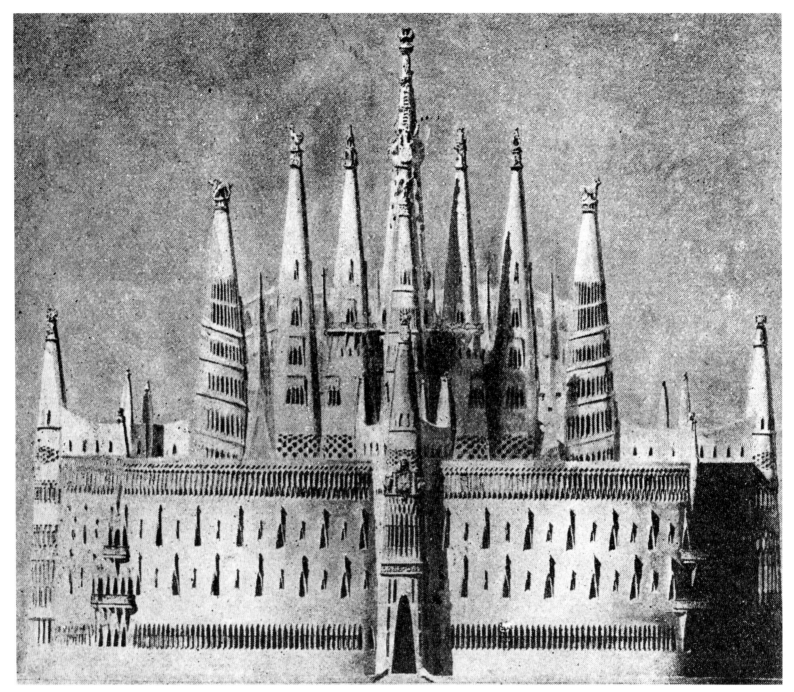

New York hotel • NEW YORK CITY • 1908

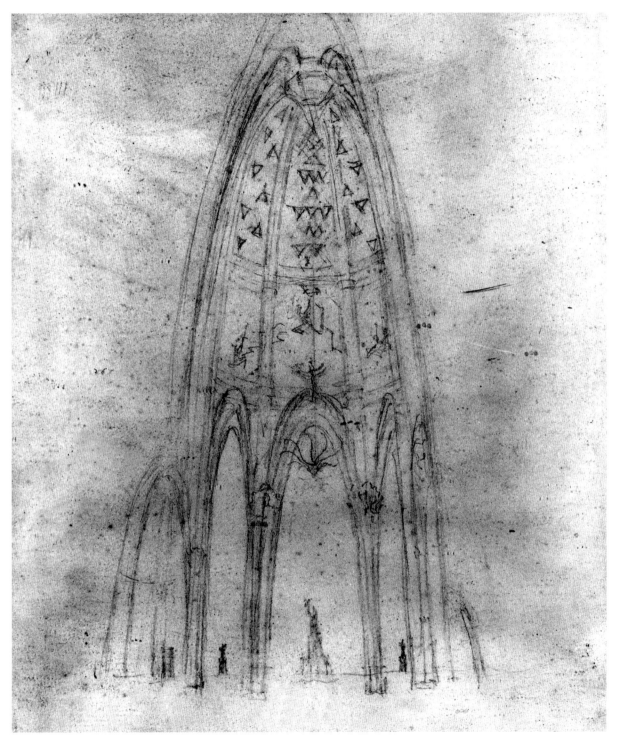

PAGE 124: The Nativity facade of the Expiatory Church of the Sagrada Familia, 1883–1926, *calle Marina*.

PAGE 125: Sea turtle on the base of a column. Charity portal of the Nativity facade of the Sagrada Familia.

OPPOSITE: Design for the Franciscan Catholic Missions.

LEFT: Sketch by Gaudí for a hotel in New York. Section of the great hall America, 1908.

Sagrada Familia • BARCELONA • 1883-1926

OPPOSITE: Portals of Faith, Charity, and Hope in the Nativity facade.

LEFT: Facade of the Passion on the side opposite the Nativity. Begun in 1956, thirty years after Gaudí's death. Sculptures by J. M. Subirachs.

RIGHT: The cypress, symbol of Christ. White doves alighting on its branches represent the souls of the blessed.

OPPOSITE: Towers of the Nativity facade with the inscription *Sanctus, Sanctus, Sanctus* from the Book of the Apocalypse.

OPPOSITE: Pinnacles of the
apse and towers of the
Passion facade.

LEFT: Tower finials with
episcopal symbols: the
miter, the crozier,
and the ring.

OPPOSITE: Interior of the Nativity facade at the end of the transept.

LEFT: The four towers of the Nativity facade along with those of the Passion and Glory facades represent the twelve apostles.

ABOVE: Stone tracery and polychrome glass windows in the central part of the Nativity facade.

OPPOSITE: Rear view of the towers of the Nativity facade seen from the facade of the Passion.

LEFT: The Coronation of the Virgin above the Charity portal.

RIGHT: The Mysteries of
the Rosary and the
Signs of the Zodiac in
sculptures and reliefs on
the Nativity facade.

OPPOSITE: Angels and
shepherds around
the Bethlehem portal,
above the Charity portal.

ABOVE: The Massacre of the Innocents on the Nativity facade.

TOP, RIGHT: The Marriage of the Virgin and Saint Joseph.

ABOVE: The Birth of Christ with the figures of the Virgin, Saint Joseph, and the Infant Christ, by the sculptor Jaime Busquets.

OPPOSITE: Jesus among the Doctors of the Law on the Nativity facade.

CHRONOLOGY

1852, June 25	Birth of Gaudí
1852, June 26	Baptism in church of Saint Peter, Reus
1863	Begins studies at the Escuelas Pías, Reus
1869	Moves to Barcelona to study architecture
1873	Enrolls in the Provincial School of Architecture, Barcelona
1876	Death of Gaudí's mother, Antonia Cornet Bertrán
1878, March 15	Degree in architecture
1879	Altar for the School of Jesus-Mary, Tarragona
1883	Begins work on the Sagrada Familia, Barcelona
1884–1887	Pavilions of the Güell Estate, Barcelona
1885, March 19	First design for the Sagrada Familia project
1886–1888	Palacio Güell, Barcelona
1887–1888	Teresian School, Barcelona
1889–1893	Episcopal Palace, Astorga
1891–1892	Casa de los Botines, León
1895–1897	Güell Cellars, Garraf, Barcelona
1898–1899	Casa Calvet, Barcelona
1900–1902	Entrance portal of the Miralles Estate, Barcelona
1900–1909	Bellesguard Tower, Barcelona
1900–1914	Park Güell
1903–1914	Restoration of the Cathedral of Mallorca
1903–1916	First Glorious Mystery, Montserrat
1904–1906	Casa Batlló, Barcelona
1906	Gaudí begins to live at the Park Güell

1906, October 29	Death of Gaudí's father, Francisco Gaudí Serra
1906–1911	Casa Milà (La Pedrera), Barcelona
1908–1917	Crypt of the Güell Estate church, Barcelona
1910	Gaudí exhibition at the Grand Palais in Paris
1912, January 11	Death of his niece, Rosa Egea Gaudí
1914	Death of his associate, Francisco Berenguer
1918, July 9	Death of Eusebio Güell
1925	Completion of the Sagrada Familia Bell Tower of Saint Barnabas
1926, June 7	Gaudí is struck by a streetcar
1926, June 10	He dies in the Santa Cruz Hospital, Barcelona
1926, June 12	He is buried in the Carmen Chapel of the Sagrada Familia crypt
1936, July 20	An intentional sacrilegious fire in the crypt and subsequent desecration of Gaudí's tomb
1939	Identification of Gaudí's body and its eventual replacement in the tomb
1952	Sagrada Familia facade of the Passion begun
1952	Centenary exhibition
1956	Royal Cátedra Gaudí created at the university
1969	The works of Gaudí declared National Monuments
1984	Three works by Gaudí entered on the World Heritage list of UNESCO: the Casa Milà, the Palacio Güell, and the Park Güell

INDEX

PICTURE CREDITS